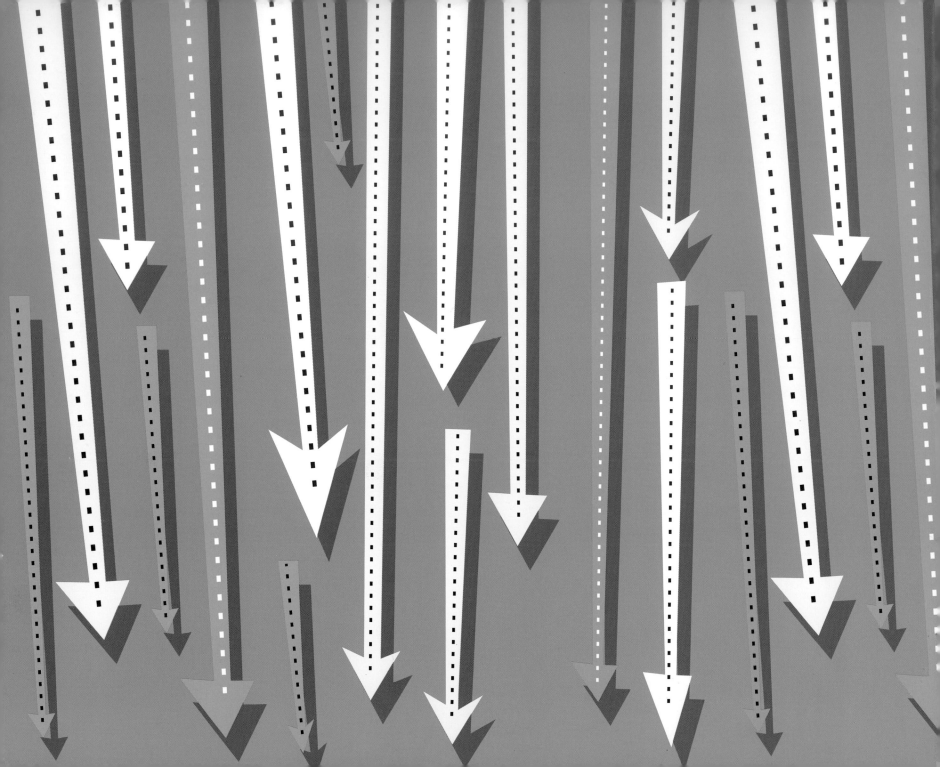

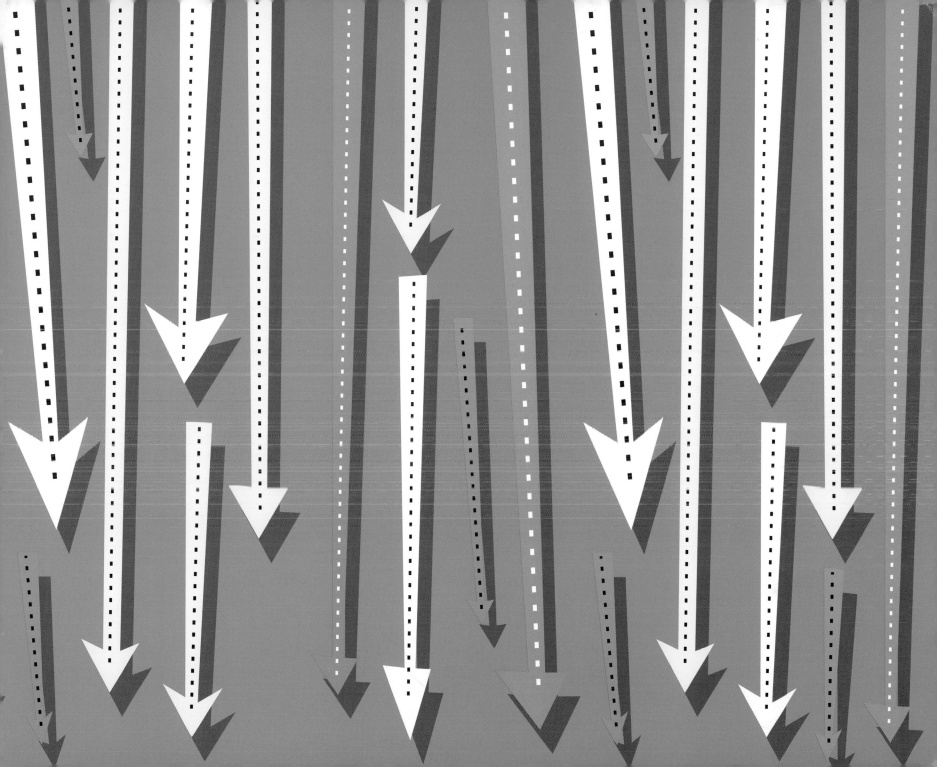

GRAVITY IS

Collins
An Imprint of HarperCollinsPublishers

LET'S-READ-AND-FIND-OUT SCIENCE®

STAGE 2

A MYSTERY

BY FRANKLYN M. BRANLEY

ILLUSTRATED BY EDWARD MILLER

To Oscar Wostenholme—E.M.

The art in this book was created using the computer.

A special thanks to David Ward for his expert review of the book.

Photos on page 4 courtesy of NASA.

The Let's-Read-and-Find-Out Science book series was originated by Dr. Franklyn M. Branley, Astronomer Emeritus and former Chairman of the American Museum–Hayden Planetarium, and was formerly co-edited by him and Dr. Roma Gans, Professor Emeritus of Childhood Education, Teachers College, Columbia University. Text and illustrations for each of the books in the series are checked for accuracy by an expert in the relevant field. For more information about Let's-Read-and-Find-Out Science books, write to HarperCollins Children's Books, 195 Broadway, New York, NY 10007, or visit our website at www.letsreadandfindout.com.

Let's Read-and-Find-Out Science® is a trademark of HarperCollins Publishers.
Collins is an imprint of HarperCollins Publishers.

Library of Congress Cataloging-in-Publication Data
Branley, Franklyn Mansfield, 1915–2002.
  Gravity is a mystery / by Franklyn M. Branley ; illustrated by Edward Miller. — 1st ed.
    p.   cm. — (Let's-read-and-find-out-science)
  Previously published: New York : T.Y. Crowell, c1986.
  ISBN-10: 0-06-028532-X (trade bdg.) — ISBN-13: 978-0-06-028532-6 (trade bdg.)
  ISBN-10: 0-06-445201-8 (pbk.) — ISBN-13: 978-0-06-445201-4 (pbk.)
  1. Gravitation—Juvenile literature. 2. Gravity—Juvenile literature. [1. Gravity.] I. Miller, Edward, 1964– ill. II. Title.
QC178.B66 2007   2006020226
531'.14—dc22   CIP
                                                                                    AC

Typography by Edward Miller

14 15 16 SCP 10 9

Newly illustrated Edition

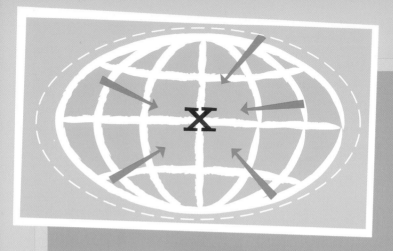

Sir Isaac Newton is the first person credited with discovering the force of gravity and how it kept objects in space (the earth and the moon) in their orbits. His theory is called the law of universal gravitational attraction.

The Law of Universal Gravitation

$$F_g = G \frac{m_1 \, m_2}{r^2}$$

r

$m_1 \qquad m_2$

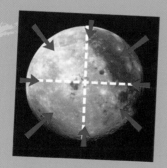

The attractive force of gravity between two particles is proportional to the product of their masses and inversely proportional to the square of the distance between them.

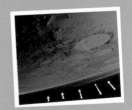

WHAT GOES UP MUST COME DOWN!

Suppose you could dig a hole to the center of the earth. Suppose you dug right past the center. If you dug long enough and deep enough, you would come out in the Indian Ocean.

North America

← center

India

Indian Ocean

If you jumped into the hole, you would fall down. Down and down you would go. You would fall faster and faster toward the center of the earth. When you reached the center, you would be going so fast you could not stop. You would go right past the center.

Then, on the other side, you would move up and away from the center of the earth. You would fall up for a while. You would go slower and slower. Then you would stop. You would almost get to the Indian Ocean—but not quite.

Now you would fall back toward the center of the earth.

You would go faster and faster, right past the center.

But you would not quite reach your starting point.

Back and forth you would go. Each time you would go a shorter distance past the center.

Back and forth, back and forth.

Gravity would make you fall toward the center of the earth. When you moved past the center, gravity would pull you back again.

After a long, long time you would stop moving. You would stay at the center of the earth.

Gravity pulls everything toward the center of the earth.

center

9

When you run downhill, gravity pulls you.

When you throw a ball up, gravity pulls it down.

10

When you sit, gravity holds you down.

When you lie down, gravity holds you to the bed.

But what is gravity?

We know gravity is everywhere, even though we can't see it. We know it pulls on every rock, every grain of sand. It pulls on everything. But no one knows exactly what gravity is. That's why we say gravity is a mystery.

The gravity of the earth pulls everything toward the center of the earth. You know this when you try to lift a heavy stone. Gravity pulls it down. The more the stone weighs, the more gravity pulls on it. To lift the stone, you must pull up harder than gravity pulls down.

You already know how much gravity pulls on you. Do you weigh 60 pounds? That means the pull of the earth's gravity on you is 60 pounds. How much you weigh tells how much gravity pulls on you. How much a stone weighs tells how much gravity pulls on the stone.

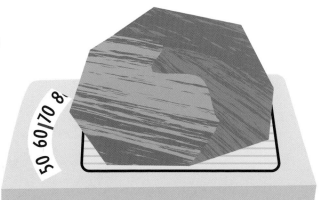

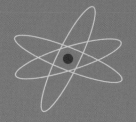

The earth has gravity, and so does the moon. If you were on the moon, the moon's gravity would pull you toward the center of the moon. The moon has less gravity than the earth has. This means the moon's gravity does not pull as hard as the earth's gravity.

Do you weigh 60 pounds? If you were on the moon, you would weigh only 10 pounds. The pull of the moon's gravity on you would only be 10 pounds.

Moon

Saturn

The earth and the moon have gravity, and so does each of
the nine planets. Jupiter and Neptune have more gravity than the
earth has. On these planets you would weigh more than you weigh on the
earth. On Neptune you would weigh only a little more. On Jupiter you would
weigh a lot more.

Do you weigh 60 pounds? On Jupiter you would weigh about 142 pounds.

Neptune

Jupiter

Gravity on Mercury, Venus, Mars, Saturn, Uranus, and Pluto is less than it is on the earth. On these planets you would weigh less than you weigh on the earth. On Venus, Saturn, and Uranus you would weigh only a little less. But on Mercury, Mars, and Pluto you would weigh a lot less.

Do you weigh 60 pounds? On Mercury and Mars you would weigh only about 23 pounds. Even less on Pluto.

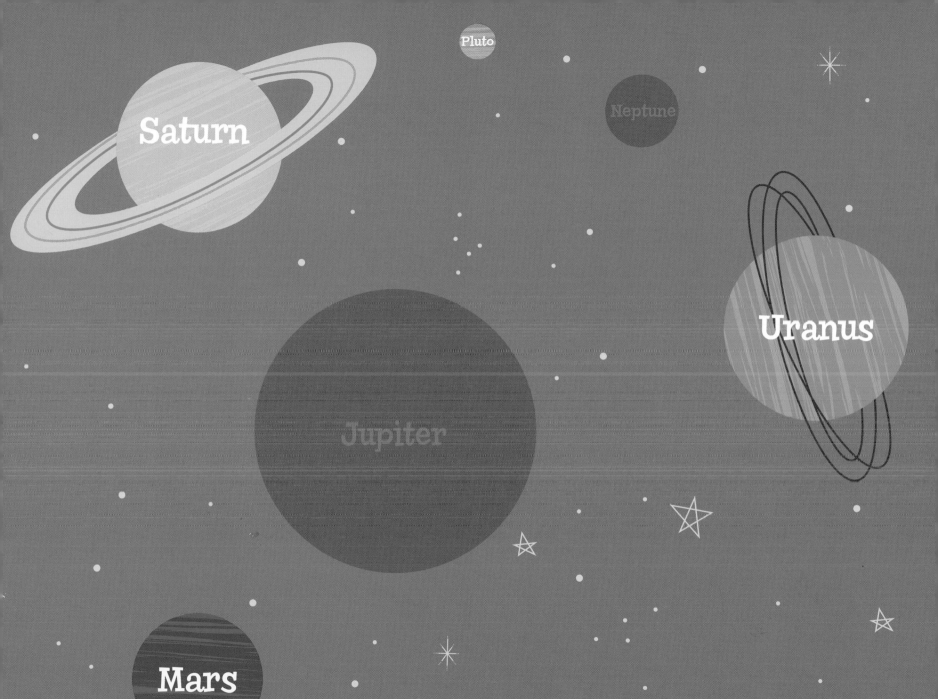

Saturn

Pluto

Neptune

Jupiter

Uranus

Mars

Mercury

Earth

Suppose you weigh 60 pounds. This is about how much you would weigh on the moon, on each of the planets, and on the sun:

Pluto	5 pounds
Moon	10 pounds
Mercury	23 pounds
Mars	23 pounds
Uranus	53 pounds
Venus	55 pounds

Sun

Venus

Saturn	. . . .	55 pounds
Earth	. . . .	60 pounds
Neptune	. . . .	67 pounds
Jupiter	. . . .	142 pounds
Sun	. . . .	1,680 pounds

Jupiter

Mars

If you were on Mars, gravity would pull you toward the center of Mars. You could stand up and sit down just as you can on the earth. It would be easier to move around, though, because you would weigh less. You could run in big giant steps because gravity on Mars is much less than it is on the earth.

You would weigh a lot more on Jupiter than you do on the earth. It would be harder to move around on that planet. Your legs would get tired from carrying you. Try running with a ninety-pound pack on your back. That's what it would be like all the time on Jupiter.

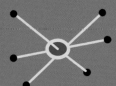

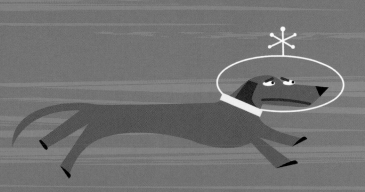

Gravity is everywhere—on the earth, on the moon, and on Jupiter, Mars, and all the other planets. The sun has gravity too, and so does every other star.

The gravity of the earth holds things on the earth. It holds down rugs and tables, and you and me.

We know where gravity is: It is everywhere.

And we know what gravity does.

But no one knows exactly what gravity is.

GRAVITY IS

A MYSTERY.

FIND OUT MORE ABOUT GRAVITY

GRAVITY ACTIVITY

Materials Needed:

Marble   Baseball   Chair   Paper   Ping-Pong ball

Find out how gravity works on objects by doing a brief experiment. If you drop a marble from one hand and a baseball from the other, which do you think would hit the ground first? Write down your answer, and then with an adult, let your gravity experiment begin.

Stand on a chair and drop a marble and a baseball from the height of your shoulder. Do they hit the ground at the same time? Repeat the process if you are unsure.

How could both objects hit the ground at the same time if the baseball is clearly bigger than the marble? Why do you think that happened?

Then drop a piece of paper and a Ping-Pong ball from atop the chair at the height of your shoulder. Did the paper take longer to reach the ground? Crumple the paper into a ball and repeat the process. Did they hit the ground at the same time?

The weight of an object doesn't determine how fast it will fall because of gravity, but its shape does. That is why the small marble and the larger baseball hit the floor at the same time, but a flat piece of paper takes longer to reach the floor than a Ping-Pong ball. The force of gravity on each object always remains the same, but the size and shape of an object can affect how fast it moves.

GRAVITY FACTS

- Your mass stays the same no matter where you are. If you are on the moon, your weight is one-sixth your weight on the earth, but your mass is exactly the same.

- The gravity of the sun is so strong that it holds all nine planets in the solar system in their orbits. Don't forget that the earth is 93 million miles away from the sun—that is a strong gravitational pull!

- Planets have a spherical shape because of gravity.

- Gravity is the weakest of the four fundamental forces of the universe.

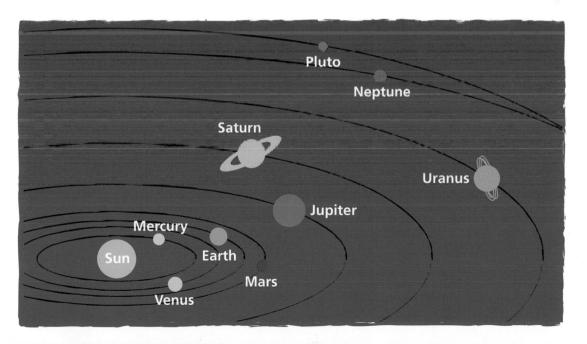

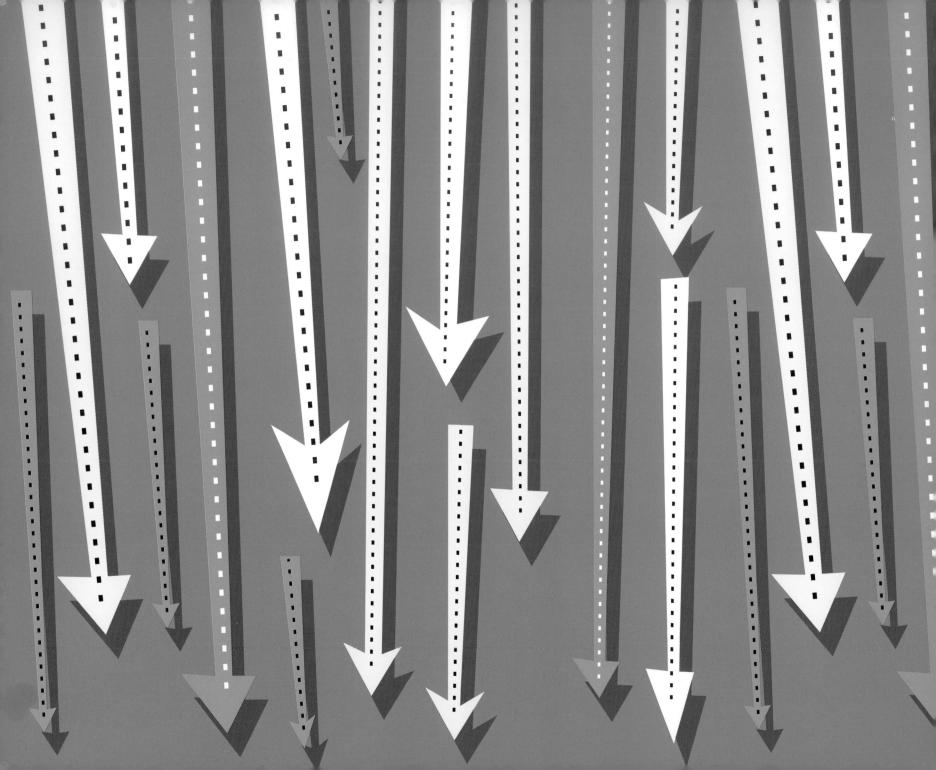

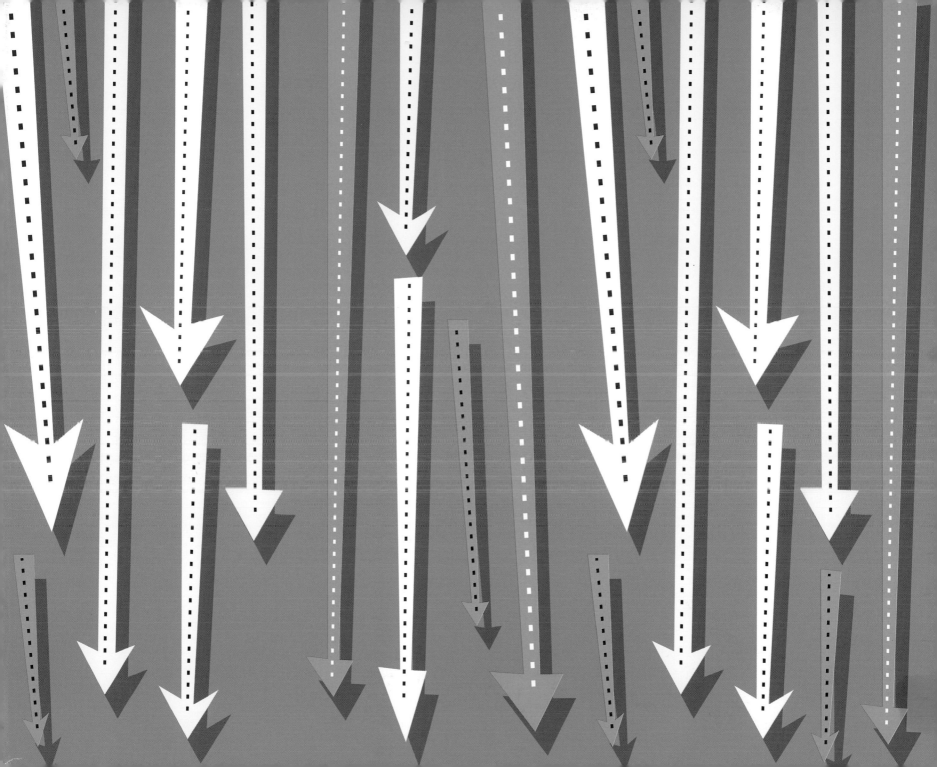